A World War II

selected by Wendy Body

Contents

Autumn journal *Louis MacNeice*	2
War rhymes *Anonymous*	4
Evacuee *Edith Pickthall*	6
Meeting *Michelle Magorian*	8
For Johnny *John Pudney*	14
For your tomorrow…	16
I never raised my boy… *Traditional*	20
Pebble *Michael Rosen*	22
Reunion *Christobel Mattingley*	24
Peace *Richard Eburne aged 12*	30
For the fallen *Laurence Binyon*	32

Autumn journal

Today was a beautiful day, the sky was
 a brilliant
Blue for the first time for weeks and weeks
But posters flapping on the railings tell
 the flustered
World that Hitler speaks, that Hitler speaks
And we cannot take it in and we go to
 our daily
Jobs to the dull refrain of the caption "War"
Buzzing around us as from hidden insects
And we think "This must be wrong, it has
 happened before,
Just like this before, we must be
 dreaming" ...

And a train begins to chug and I wonder what the morning
Paper will say
And decide to go quickly to sleep for the morning already
Is with us, the day is today.

from *'Autumn journal'* by Louis MacNeice

War rhymes

(used for skipping or chanting by children)

Underneath the churchyard, six feet deep,
There lies Hitler fast asleep,
All the little mice come and tickle his feet,
'Neath the churchyard, six feet deep.

Who's that knocking at the window?
Who's that knocking at the door?
If it's Hitler, let him in
And we'll sit him on a pin,
And we won't see old Hitler any more.

Anonymous

Evacuee

The slum had been his home since he
 was born;
And then war came, and he was
 rudely torn
From all he'd ever known; and with
 his case
Of mean necessities, brought to a place
Of silences and space; just boom of sea
And sough of wind; small wonder then
 that he

Crept out one night to seek his sordid slum,
And thought to find his way. By dawn
　he'd come
A few short miles; and cattle in their herds
Gazed limpidly as he trudged by, and birds
Just stirring in first light, awoke to hear
His lonely sobbing, born of abject fear
Of sea and hills and sky; of silent night
Unbroken by the sound of shout and fight.

　　　　　　　　　　　　Edith Pickthall

Meeting

"Yes," said Tom bluntly, on opening the front door. "What d'you want?"

A harassed middle-aged woman in a green coat and felt hat stood on his step. He glanced at the armband on her sleeve. She gave him an awkward smile.

"I'm the Billeting Officer for this area," she began.

"Oh yes, and what's that got to do wi' me?"

She flushed slightly. "Well, Mr, Mr…"

"Oakley. Thomas Oakley."

"Ah, thank you, Mr Oakley." She paused and took a deep breath. "Mr Oakley, with the declaration of war imminent..."

Tom waved his hand. "I knows all that. Git to the point. What d'you want?" He noticed a small boy at her side.

"It's him I've come about," she said. "I'm on my way to your village hall with the others."

"What others?"

She stepped to one side. Behind the large iron gate which stood at the end of the graveyard were a small group of children. Many of them were filthy and very poorly clad. Only a handful had a blazer or coat. They all looked bewildered and exhausted. One tiny dark-haired girl in the front was hanging firmly on to a new teddy-bear.

The woman touched the boy at her side and pushed him forward.

"There's no need to tell me," said Tom. "It's obligatory and it's for the war effort."

"You are entitled to choose your child, I know," began the woman apologetically.

Tom gave a snort.

"But," she continued. "his mother wants him to be with someone who's religious or near a church. She was quite adamant. Said she would only let him be evacuated if he was."

"Was what?" asked Tom impatiently.

"Near a church."

Tom took a second look at the child. The boy was thin and sickly-looking, pale with limp sandy hair and dull grey eyes.

"His name's Willie," said the woman.

Willie, who had been staring at the ground, looked up. Round his neck, hanging from a piece of string, was a cardboard label. It read "William Beech".

Tom was well into his sixties, a healthy, robust, stockily-built man with a head of thick white hair. Although he was of average height, in Willie's eyes he was a towering giant with skin like coarse, wrinkled brown paper and a voice like thunder.

He glared at Willie. "You'd best come in," he said abruptly.

from *Goodnight Mr Tom* by Michelle Magorian

For Johnny

Do not despair
For Johnny-Head-in-Air;
He sleeps as sound
As Johnny-underground.

Fetch out no shroud
For Johnny-in-the-Cloud,
And keep your tears
For him in after years.

Better by far
For Johnny-the-bright-star
To keep your head
And see his children fed.

John Pudney

For your tomorrow

*When you go home tell them of us and say
For your tomorrow we gave our today.*

Sergeant Hubert Frank Moroni, known always as Mac, was aged 21 when he died. He was killed a week before he was due to be married.

Aged 3½

Aged 6

Aged 12

29 February 1944

...your son, Sergeant Hubert Frank Moroni, Royal Air Force, is missing as a result of air operations on 20th February 1944, when a Lancaster aircraft in which he was flying as mid-upper gunner set out to bomb Leipzig and was not heard from again...

DEEPLY REGRET TO ADVISE YOU THAT ACCORDING TO INFORMATION RECEIVED THROUGH THE INTERNATIONAL RED CROSS COMMITTEE YOUR SON SGT HUBERT FRANK MORONI IS BELIEVED TO HAVE LOST HIS LIFE...

Telegram from Air Ministry, 19th April 1944

21 April 1944

...The Committee's telegram, quoting official German information, states that your son and the six other occupants of the aircraft in which he was flying that night were killed on 20th February. It contains no information regarding the place of their burial...

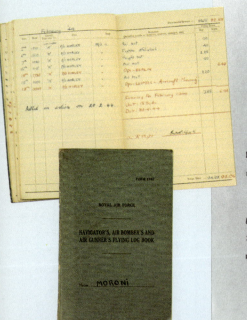

BUCKINGHAM PALACE

    The Queen and I offer you our heartfelt sympathy in your great sorrow.

    We pray that your country's gratitude for a life so nobly given in its service may bring you some measure of consolation.

George R.I.

F. Moroni, Esq.

3RD JANUARY 1948

...WAS BURIED BY THE GERMANS IN THE CEMETERY AT JENA. HIS REMAINS HAVE BEEN REVERENTLY REINTERRED IN THE BRITISH MILITARY CEMETERY AT HEERSTRASSE, BERLIN, WHERE HE NOW RESTS WITH HIS COMRADES IN ADJOINING GRAVES. IT IS FELT THAT OUR FALLEN SHOULD NOT BE LEFT IN ISOLATED CEMETERIES THROUGHOUT GERMANY, BUT SHOULD REST TOGETHER IN SPECIAL MILITARY CEMETERIES, THE SOIL OF WHICH WILL ALWAYS BE BRITISH. THESE CEMETERIES HAVE BEEN SELECTED FOR THE NATURAL BEAUTY AND PEACE OF THEIR SURROUNDINGS.

Telegram received 13th February 1944

I never raised my boy to be a soldier
I brought him up to be my pride and joy.
Who dares to lay a gun upon his shoulder,
And teach him how to kill another
　mother's boy.

I never raised my boy to be a soldier.
I brought him up to stay at home with me.
There would be no war today, if every
   mother would say
I never raised my boy to be a soldier.

Traditional North Country

Pebble

I know a man who's got a pebble.

He found it and he sucked it
during the war.
He found it and he sucked it
when they ran out of water.
He found it and he sucked it
when they were dying for a drink.
And he sucked it and he sucked it
for days and days and days.

I know a man who's got a pebble
and he keeps it in his drawer.

It's small and brown – nothing much to
    look at
but I think of the things he thinks
when he sees it:
how he found it
how he sucked it
how he nearly died for water to drink.

A small brown pebble
tucked under his tongue
and he keeps it in his drawer
to look at now and then.

Michael Rosen

Reunion

Lena's family were moved to many different camps during the war. Her father was separated from them and they have not seen him for several years. The war is now over...

Back at the camp our mother was hunting for us. "Where have you been?" she asked me. "And where is your sister?" And her voice was as shrill as the wind through the cracks in the walls of our hut.

The snow came down in the night and in the morning all the valley was white and hushed. Then over the mountainside we could see the first of the searching people for the day arriving, coming down the slope like ants. And suddenly across the snow I could hear a mouth-organ.

"It's Father!" I called.

And I ran. And ran. Shouting. Falling in the snow drifts. Laughing. Crying. I was the first to reach him. And he hugged me. And hugged me. And hugged me.

Then my sister came. And he hugged her.

And my mother. And they hugged each other.

And we all hugged each other.

Till Father said, "Careful. We don't want to break the other wing".

And he pulled something out of his pocket. I thought it would be a bird – a blue tit or a goldfinch.

But it was a fragment of glass. And in the glass there was an angel. Blue as the sky and gold as the Sun.

My sister fingered the sharp edges. "Its wing is broken," she said sadly.

"But look!" I said. "It's playing a mouth-organ!"

"You could say so," Father laughed.

"Where did you find it?" Mother asked.

"In the ruins of a church," Father said. "And it's kept me company all the time I've been searching for you."

"And how did you find us?"

Father laughed again. "Whenever I went into a camp, I played my mouth-organ. And children used to come up to me and say, 'Those are the songs Lena and Anna used to sing. You must be their father. They said you had one arm and played the mouth-organ.' So I knew I'd find you somewhere, some day."

My sister said, "Can we go home now?" And our mother asked it with her eyes.

But our father shook his head. "There's no home to go to. And other people have taken our land."

My sister said, "It's not fair. After everything…"

But our father put his mouth-organ to her lips and her words turned into funny sounds. And we all laughed.

"We'll find another home," our father said. "You'll see."

And we did. Though it took a long while…

from *The Angel With a Mouth Organ* by Christobel Mattingley

Peace

War is full of people dying,
War is full of relatives crying,
Peace makes people happy, not sad,
Things like Peace are good, not bad.

War is dismal, dark and bloody,
In trenches deep, but small and muddy.
Peace is beautiful, quiet and clean,
When people are kind, no one is mean.

War is terrible, no matter what kind,
Peace is a lot nicer, I'm sure you'll find.
Peace and happiness come hand in hand,
Sparkling and golden like the desert sand.

Peace and joy are like a team,
Each one like a bright sunbeam.

Richard Eburne, aged 12

For the fallen

They shall grow not old, as we that are left grow old:
Age shall not weary them, nor the years condemn.
At the going down of the Sun and in the morning
We will remember them.

from '*For the fallen*' by Laurence Binyon